FOREST FEELINGS

JIMMY THE BLUE JAY FEELS JEALOUS

by Megan Atwood
illustrated by Carissa Harris

Tools for Parents & Teachers

Grasshopper Books enhance imagination and introduce the earliest readers to fiction with fun storylines and illustrations. The easy-to-read text supports early reading experiences with repetitive sentence patterns and sight words.

Before Reading

- Discuss the cover illustration. What do they see?
- Look at the picture glossary together. Discuss the words.

Read the Book

- Read the book to the child, or have him or her read independently.
- "Walk" through the book and look at the illustrations. Who is the main character? What is happening in the story?

After Reading

- Prompt the child to think more. Ask: Jimmy feels jealous. How do we know? What does he say and do that show he is jealous?

Grasshopper Books are published by Jump!
5357 Penn Avenue South
Minneapolis, MN 55419
www.jumplibrary.com

Library of Congress Cataloging-in-Publication Data

Names: Atwood, Megan, author.
Harris, Carissa, illustrator.
Title: Jimmy the blue jay feels jealous / by Megan Atwood; illustrated by Carissa Harris.
Description: Minneapolis, MN: Jump!, Inc., 2024.
Series: Forest feelings | Includes index.
Audience: Ages 7–10.
Identifiers: LCCN 2023029079 (print)
LCCN 2023029080 (ebook)
ISBN 9798889969631 (hardcover)
ISBN 9798889969648 (paperback)
ISBN 9798889969655 (ebook)
Subjects: CYAC: Jealousy—Fiction. | Blue jays—Fiction.
Crow family (Birds)—Fiction. | LCGFT: Animal fiction.
Picture books.
Classification: LCC PZ7.A8952 Ji 2024 (print)
LCC PZ7.A8952 (ebook)
DDC [E]—dc23
LC record available at https://lccn.loc.gov/2023029079
LC ebook record available at https://lccn.loc.gov/2023029080

Editor: Jenna Gleisner
Direction and Layout: Molly Ballanger
Illustrator: Carissa Harris

Printed in the United States of America at
Corporate Graphics in North Mankato, Minnesota.

Table of Contents

A Spot of His Own

Jimmy the blue jay lives in a big oak tree. He loves to eat acorns.

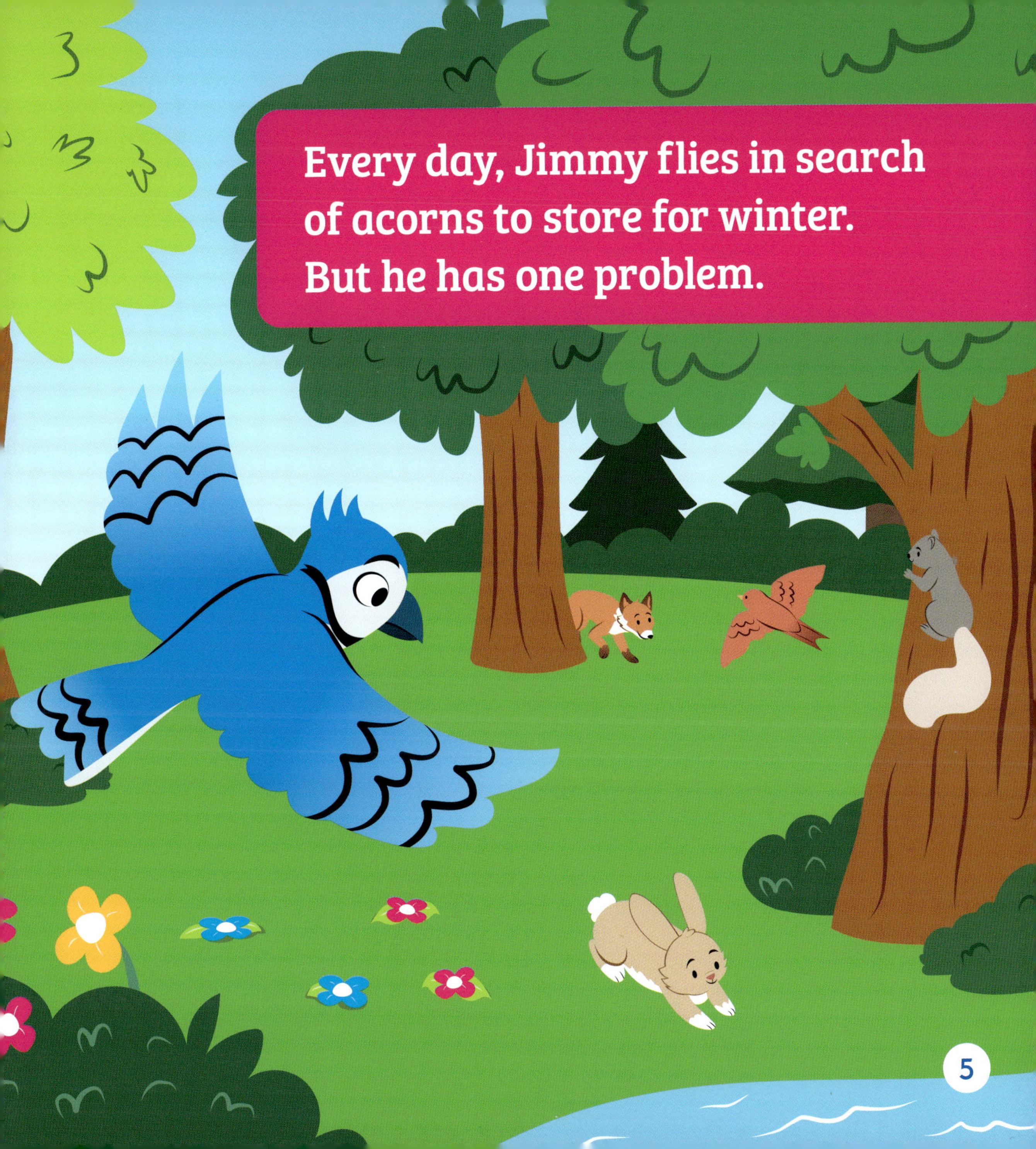

Every day, Jimmy flies in search of acorns to store for winter. But he has one problem.

He hasn't found a place to store them!

Jimmy watches Janessa store her acorns under a bush. Jamal hides his in a hole in a tree.

Jimmy is the only jay without a hiding spot. He feels left out.

Jimmy flies to Jamal's tree.

"Can I store my acorns here?" he asks.

"This is my spot. Find your own, Jimmy," Jamal squawks.

Jimmy feels frustrated. He flies away.

Next, Jimmy asks Janessa.

"Can I store my acorns here?"

Janessa flaps her wings and shoos Jimmy away.

Jimmy feels jealous. His friends have something he does not.

His body feels tense. He clenches his beak tight. He feels like he is about to burst.

Just then, he sees Jamal fly away. Jimmy flies as fast as he can to Jamal's tree!

This will be a great spot for MY acorns, Jimmy thinks to himself as he throws Jamal's acorns to the ground.

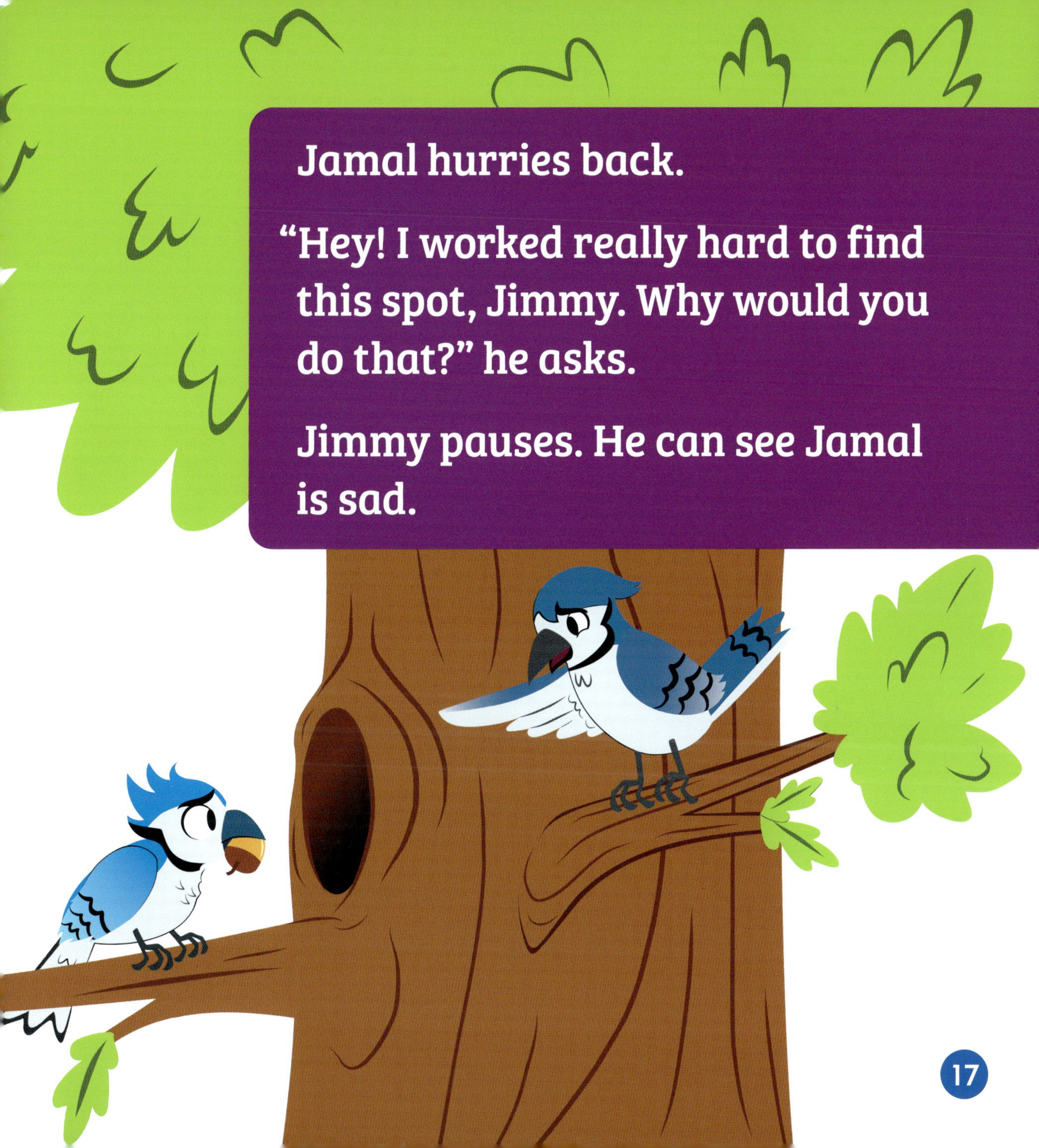

Jamal hurries back.

“Hey! I worked really hard to find this spot, Jimmy. Why would you do that?” he asks.

Jimmy pauses. He can *see* Jamal is sad.

He puts the acorns back.

“I’m sorry, Jamal. I was jealous and really wanted a spot,” says Jimmy.

“It’s OK. I feel jealous sometimes, too,” Jamal says.

Jimmy flies to a new tree to think. He did not like feeling jealous.

He looks up. Then his face lights up.

He finds a hiding spot!

Let's Review!

Look at the scenes below. Point to those that show Jimmy jealous. How do you know?

Picture Glossary

clenches
Closes tightly.

frustrated
Feeling helpless or discouraged.

shoos
Scares, drives, or sends away.

squawks
Makes a loud, harsh screech.

store
To put things away to use later.

tense
Stretched stiff and tight.

Index

To Learn More

Finding more information is as easy as 1, 2, 3.

1. Go to www.factsurfer.com
2. Enter "**Jimmythebluejayfeelsjealous**" into the search box.
3. Choose your book to see a list of websites.